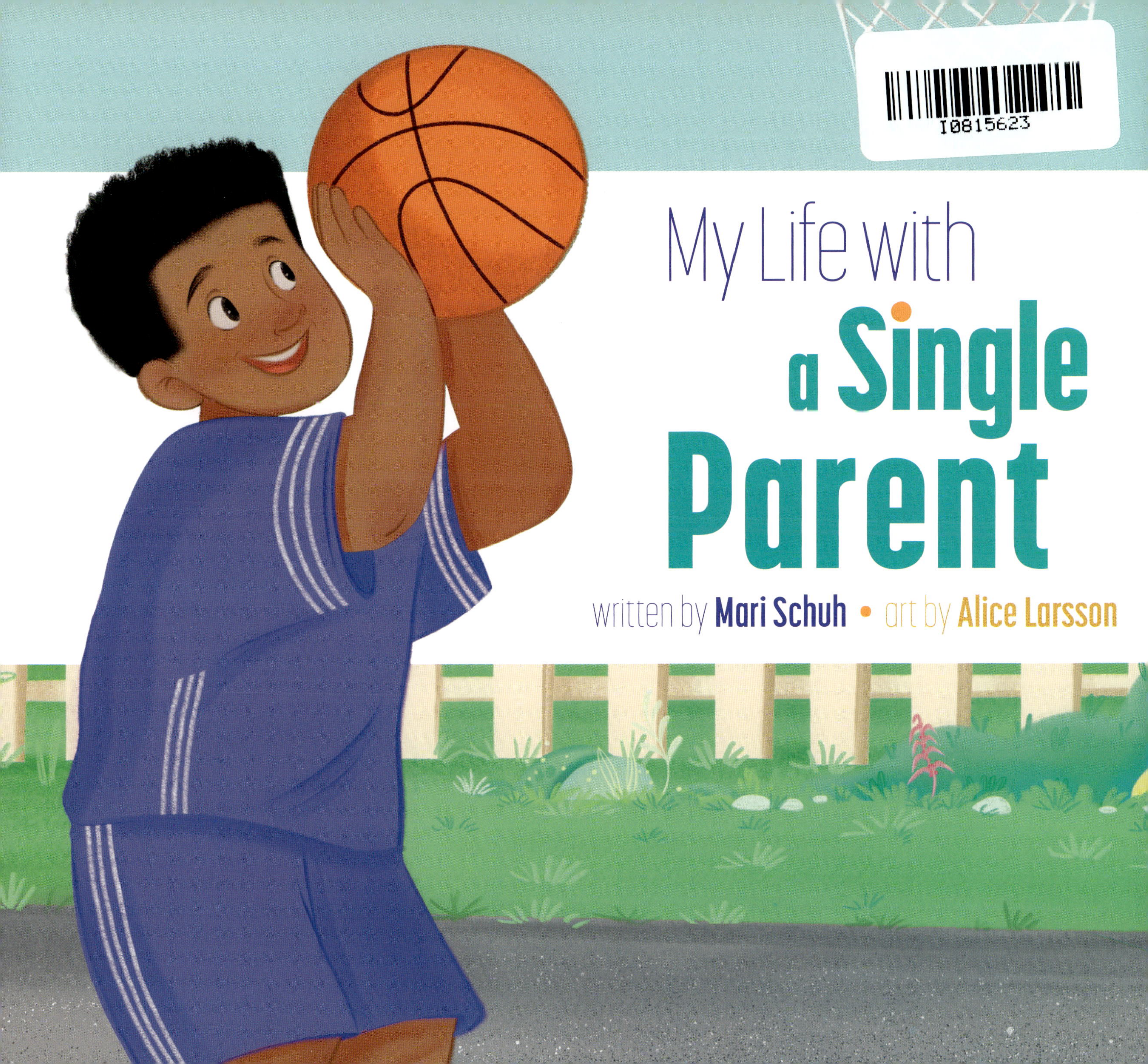

My Life with a Single Parent

written by Mari Schuh • art by Alice Larsson

AMICUS ILLUSTRATED
is published by Amicus Learning, an imprint of Amicus
P.O. Box 227, Mankato, MN 56002
www.amicuspublishing.us

Editor: Rebecca Glaser
Series Designer: Kathleen Petelinsek
Book Designer: Emily Dietz

Library of Congress Cataloging-in-Publication Data
Names: Schuh, Mari C., 1975- author | Larsson, Alice illustrator
Title: My life with a single parent / by Mari Schuh ; illustrated by Alice Larsson.
Description: Mankato, MN : Amicus Learning, an imprint of Amicus, [2026] | Series: My life with... | Includes bibliographical references. | Audience: Ages 6-9 | Audience: Grades 2-3 | Summary: "Asher adjusts to life with a single parent after his parents' separation. Despite challenges, he finds joy in spending time with both parents. Includes tips for respecting kids with single parents and a glossary of important terms"—Provided by publisher.
Identifiers: LCCN 2025014236 (print) | LCCN 2025014237 (ebook) | ISBN 9798892008884 library binding | ISBN 9798892009546 paperback | ISBN 9798896850205 ebook
Subjects: LCSH: Children of single parents—Juvenile literature | Single-parent families—Juvenile literature | Divorced parents—Juvenile literature
Classification: LCC HQ777.4 .S35 2026 (print) | LCC HQ777.4 (ebook) | DDC 306.85/6—dc23/eng/20250512
LC record available at https://lccn.loc.gov/2025014236
LC ebook record available at https://lccn.loc.gov/2025014237

Printed in China

About the Author
Mari Schuh's love of reading began with cereal boxes at the kitchen table. Today she is the author of hundreds of nonfiction books for beginning readers. With each book, Mari hopes she's helping kids learn a little bit more about the world around them. Find out more about her at marischuh.com.

About the Illustrator
Alice Larsson is a London-based illustrator originally from Sweden. A natural creative, she is thrilled to be able to connect characters and stories through her work. Outside of drawing, Alice loves spending time with family and friends, as well as reading books and traveling, which sparks her creativity.

Hey there! My name is Asher. We probably have a lot in common. I like to play basketball. I also like to program computer games and use my 3D printer. We might be different, too. My mom is a single parent. Let me tell you about my life.

When I was five years old, my mom and dad separated. My mom, my sister, and I moved to an apartment nearby.

My mom and dad got a divorce when I was eight years old. Then later, my dad moved to another city. This means I don't get to see him as often, which sometimes makes me sad. But he visits me often, and we talk all the time.

During the divorce, I talked to a therapist. She listened to me talk about my emotions. She let me draw, too. She helped me feel better.

My mom is the only parent in our home. She has to do most of the work herself. To save time, she has groceries delivered to our home. I help mom put away the groceries.

My grandma helps, too. Sometimes she helps my mom make dinner for us.

I help in other ways, too, even if I don’t always enjoy chores. I take out the trash and the recycling.

I take our dog for walks. I feed her and give her water, too.

Mom is busy. She teaches at a university. But she always has time for me and my sister. Mom goes to all my basketball games. She teaches me how to bake and cook. She also helps me learn to play the violin.

When I'm with my dad, my mom usually stays home. She gets lots of work done.

Other times, she has fun shopping or getting her nails done.

Mom has taught me to have a positive attitude. I focus on all the good things in my life. I know that Mom and Dad both love me. Sometimes all four of us still go places together.

Mom takes good care of me. She makes sure I have everything I need. This makes me feel good. I always try my best. Mom is proud of me, and I am proud of her!

Meet Asher

Hello! I'm Asher. I live in Florida with my mom and my younger sister. We have a dog named Chia. I like to play video games and play my violin. Learning how to cook is also fun. My favorite color is purple. When I grow up, I want to be a lawyer or a pro basketball player.

Respecting Kids Who Live with a Single Parent

A kid with a single parent might go back and forth between two homes. If their plans change and they can't play with you, be understanding. Try to find a new time that works for both of you.

Remember that there are all kinds of families. Every family is unique. What works for some families does not work for others.

Every family has its own activities, rules, and traditions. This is true for single-parent families, too.

Divorce is not a kid's fault. Do not blame kids for their parents' divorce.

Be a good listener if your friend wants to talk about their family. If they don't want to talk, respect their privacy.

Helpful Terms

attitude A way of thinking about something.

divorce The ending of a marriage by a court.

emotions Strong feelings such as love, sadness, fear, and happiness.

proud Feeling pleased and happy with yourself or another person.

separated Not living together.

single parent A parent who lives with one or more children and no husband or wife.

therapist A person who is trained to help people to learn new skills when they have conditions, disorders, illnesses, and tough times in their life.

Read More

Finne, Stephanie. ***Parents and Guardians.*** Minneapolis: Jump!, Inc., 2025.

Peterson, Christy. ***Many Ways to Be a Family.*** Minneapolis: Lerner Publications, 2023.

Schuh, Mari. ***My Life with Divorced Parents.*** My Life With... Mankato, Minn.: Amicus Publishing, 2025.

Websites

CBC KIDS: DIFFERENT TYPES OF FAMILIES

https://www.cbc.ca/kids/articles/there-are-different-types-of-families

Visit this website to read about many types of families.

KIDSHEALTH: COPING WITH DIVORCE

https://kidshealth.org/en/kids/divorce-cope.html

Learn how to deal with sadness people might feel during a divorce.

SESAME WORKSHOP: TRANSITIONING BETWEEN PARENTS

https://sesameworkshop.org/resources/transitioning-between-parents/

Read this online storybook about kids whose parents live apart.